For Samantha,
    You are more than I ever could have hoped for.
                                    I Love You.
                                        ~ Daddy

You're so small and sweet
but not ready to talk.

If only I knew
what you wanted to say.

If daddy spoke baby
I'd know what you said!

"I love you"
"I'm hungry"
or "Put me to bed!"

If daddy spoke baby
I'd know you want food.

And not that you're tired
or in a bad mood.

If daddy spoke baby
and you wanted a drink.

BA BA

If daddy spoke baby
I'd know what was wrong.

This trick would be handy
Oh yes, indeed!

But daddy speaks grown up
so I'll teach you my words.

By singing and reading
of stars, clouds, and birds.

And one of these days
when you start to talk.

We'll chat and we'll laugh
while on a long walk.

So until your first word
I will patiently wait.

And I'll listen and learn
and try to translate.

And when I can't tell
if you're silly or sad